ANIMALS ARE AMAZING

GIRAFFES

BY VALERIE BODDEN

W
FRANKLIN WATTS
LONDON•SYDNEY

D0248606

Franklin Watts
First published in Great Britain in 2015 by
The Watts Publishing Group

Copyright © 2009 Creative Education,
an imprint of the Creative Company
www.thecreativecompany.us

Credits
Series Designer: The Design Lab
Art Direction: Rita Marshall
Photographs by Corbis (Theo Allofs, Jerry Cooke,
Nigel J. Dennis/Gallo Images), Dreamstime (Jenny),
Getty Images (Richard Du Toit, Suzi Eszterhas,
Gerald Hinde, George F. Mobley/National
Geographic), iStockphoto (Dirk Freder, Dieter
Hawlan, Emin Kuliyev, Christian Musat, Thomas
Polen, Eliza Snow, Rick Wylie)

Every attempt has been made to clear copyright.
Should there be any inadvertent omission please
apply to the publisher for rectification.

Dewey number: 599.638
HB ISBN: 978 1 4451 4521 1

Printed in China

Franklin Watts
An imprint of
Hachette Children's Group
Part of The Watts Publishing Group
Carmelite House
50 Victoria Embankment
London EC4Y 0DZ

An Hachette UK Company
www.hachette.co.uk

www.franklinwatts.co.uk

CONTENTS

What are giraffes?   4
Giraffe facts   7
Tall giraffes   8
Where giraffes live   11
Giraffe food   12
New giraffes   15
Giraffe talk   16
Eating and sleeping   19
Giraffes and people   20
A giraffe story   22
Useful information   24

What are giraffes?

Both male and female giraffes have two 'horns' on their heads.

Giraffes are tall **mammals** with a slim body and four long legs. They have very long necks. There are nine kinds of giraffe in the world.

mammals animals that have warm blood and hair or fur. Mammals drink milk from their mothers when they are babies.

Giraffe facts

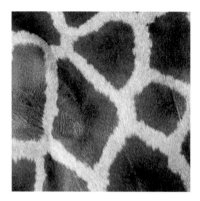

All giraffes have pale yellow or white fur, with brown patches called spots.

Giraffes have the longest necks of any animal in the world, but they have the same number of neck bones as a person! No two giraffes have the same **pattern** of spots on their fur.

pattern the way shapes and colours are arranged.

Tall giraffes

Giraffes are the tallest animals on land. They can grow up to 6 metres tall. If a giraffe stood next to a house, it could look into a window on the first floor! Giraffes are heavy animals. They weigh around 1,000 kilogrammes – about as much as a car.

Giraffes can run fast, at speeds of up to 50 kilometres per hour.

Where giraffes live

*Africa is a large, hot **continent**. It lies between South America and Asia.*

Giraffes live on the continent of Africa. All giraffes live in areas where trees can grow. Some giraffes live in forests and other giraffes live on wide grasslands.

continent one of Earth's seven big pieces of land.

Giraffe food

A giraffe's tongue is purple, black or blue in colour!

Giraffes are herbivores.

They eat twigs and leaves, which they pull off trees with their long, strong tongues. Giraffes eat about 35 kilogrammes of food every day. Giraffes do not drink a lot of water. Most of the water they need is inside the leaves they eat.

herbivores animals that only eat plants.

New giraffes

A female giraffe gives birth to her **calf** standing up. The calf falls to the ground. When it is born it is already as tall as a person – 1.8 metres tall! The day after it is born a calf is able to run. Wild giraffes can live for up to 25 years.

Female giraffes usually give birth to one calf at a time. Twins are very **rare***.*

calf a baby giraffe.
rare something that doesn't happen very often.

Giraffe talk

Giraffes live in groups, called herds, of about ten giraffes. Giraffes make lots of noises. They can grunt, snort, hiss, bleat and moo. This is how giraffes 'talk' to each other.

Giraffes have good **senses**. *They have big eyes and can see and smell very well. They use their senses to watch out for* **predators**.

senses what animals and people use to find out about the world around them. The five main senses are sight, smell, taste, touch and hearing.
predators animals (such as lions) that kill and eat other animals.

Eating and sleeping

Giraffes will drink water if they find it, but it's hard for them to reach the ground, even with such a long neck!

Giraffes spend most of their time eating. They do not sleep very much. When they do sleep, it is for only a few minutes at a time. Giraffes can lie down, but they find it easier to eat and sleep standing up. Giraffes eat and sleep both in the day and at night.

Giraffes and people

People around the world like to look at giraffes. Many zoos and safari parks keep giraffes. Some people go to see giraffes in the wild. In some places, people can even feed the giraffes. It is fun to get close to these tall animals!

In the past, few people had ever seen a real giraffe. These giraffes lived at Central Park Zoo, USA in 1939. They were popular with visitors.

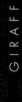

A giraffe story

Why do giraffes have such long necks? People in Africa tell a story about this. They said that the giraffe once looked like a deer and ate grass. One year, there was not enough rain and all the grass dried up. The giraffe looked up and saw some juicy leaves on a tall tree. He was hungry and wanted to eat them. He asked a magic man to help him. The man made the giraffe's neck and legs grow very long. Now the giraffe could reach the leaves and eat all he wanted!

Useful information

Read More

Awesome African Animals: Giraffes are Awesome! by Lisa J. Amstutz (Raintree, 2015)

Animal Lives: Giraffes by Sally Morgan (QED Publishing, 2014)

Websites

http://gowild.wwf.org.uk/regions/africa-games-and-activities/animal-cards
This WWF website has a section on African animals. There are lots of fun activities and stories to read, including an African animal card-making activity. Download the free templates of a giraffe and other animals for your cards.

http://www.activityvillage.co.uk/search-results?_q=giraffe
This website has lots of giraffe-inspired crafts.

http://animals.nationalgeographic.com/animals/mammals/giraffe/
The National Geographic website has useful facts and some lovely pictures of giraffes.

Every effort has been made by the Publishers to ensure that these websites are suitable for children, that they are of the highest educational value and that they contain no inappropriate or offensive material. However, because of the nature of the Internet, it is impossible to guarantee that the contents of these sites will not be altered. We strongly advise that Internet access is supervised by a responsible adult.

Index

Africa 11, 22
calves 15
food 12, 19, 20, 22

fur 7
herds 16
legs 4, 7, 22
necks 4, 7, 19, 22
safari parks 21
size 4, 8, 15

sleeping 19
sounds 16
tongues 12
trees 11, 12, 22
water 12, 19
zoos 21